GUIDE FOR BEGINNERS IN HOSPITALITY INDUSTRY

YASH NIGAM & YASH GOYAL

XpressPublishing
An imprint of Notion Press

No.8, 3rd Cross Street,CIT Colony,
Mylapore, Chennai, Tamil Nadu-600004

ISBN 978-1-63606-807-7

Contents

Acknowledgment

The world is a better place thanks to people who want to develop and lead others. What makes it even better are people who share the gift of their time to mentor future leaders. Thank you to everyone who strives to grow and help others grow.

To all the individuals we have had the opportunity to lead, be led by, or watch their leadership from afar, we want to say thank you for being the inspiration for us.

Without the support of each other, i.e. we the authors, this book would not exist. We have given each other the opportunity to lead a great group of individuals. Our ideas and suggestions helped us get to a manuscript that made us say, **"Yes, it's finally a book!"**.

Yash Nigam,a 20 years old passionate boy, born and bought up in Uttar Pradesh. He is currently pursuing Bachelor's Degree in Hospitality and Hotel Administration from Institute of Hotel Management, Lucknow.

He loves to help others also considers as his hobby. He was also selected in State Level Cricket Team while he was 18.

He has also completed the management courses from Oxford HSC.

He has a keen interest in Food and Beverage Department and wants to be a success hotelier in future.

To reach him, you can connect him through his Instagram handle (@nigam5760) also you can connect through mail i.e. yashpasha123@gmail.com.

Author 2

Yash Goyal,is 18 years old and has his roots in Madhya Pradesh. He is pursuing his Bachelor's Degree in Hospitality and Hotel Administration from IHM, Lucknow.

He has also completed the courses of Marketing and Advertising, Digital Marketing, Entrepreneurship and Event Management from @mycaptain app.

He has keen interest in Football and wants to be an successful Entrepreneur. He has worked as a co-author in his last two books and this is his first book as an author.

To reach him, you can connect through his personal Instagram handle @goyalyash024 and via Email i.e. goyalyash028@gmail.com.

Index

1

PRECISION (What is Hospitality & Hotel Management)

"How May I help you ! " (The tagline for an successful Hotelier or popularly known as Mool Mantra of the Industry for which we work.)

We are so lucky as we all got the opportunity to help others and this is the best blessing for anyone. And this is On what our Industry works!

When I was in 8th standard what Hotel Management meant to me, is a place which is full of enjoyable life with no or less work. A life which is more lavish that one can think of.

When I was in 11th standard I continued with the same mindset, but when I was in the process of getting enrolled in this industry my mind-set changed and grew bigger and bigger and changed my whole thinking.

According to books, Hospitality is:

• The quality or disposition of receiving and treating guests and strangers in a warm, friendly, generous way.

• The activity or business of providing services to guests in "Hotels, Restaurants, Bars, etc."

· Welcoming our brothers and sisters with care and willingness must not be limited to extraordinary occasions but must become for all believers a habit of service in their daily lives.

· Making others feel comfortable and welcome in your home.

According to books, Hotel Management is:

· It is closely associated with the travel industry and the hospitality industry, although there are notable differences in scope.

· It refers to the application of management concepts and structured leadership in the areas of accommodation, dining and general guest services.

But since every person's mind-set is different so What Hospitality means to us is explained as: The Hospitality Industry was born out of casual arrangements between locals and weary travellers looking for a safe place to rest their horses and lay their heads. Back then, the definition of Hospitality usually meant basic meal and some ale. These casual stays then evolved to become more than just a place to stay. Serving an increasingly-mobile class of merchants, nobles, scholars, and priests, the hospitality industry was born.

If Hospitality is discussed in detail, then it can be described in following points:-

· Hospitality is about trust and empowering staff, first and foremost.

· Hospitality is about touchpoints and micro-experiences that make each guest feel valued and at "**HOME.**" · Hospitality is about building something greater than the sum of its parts.

You walk into a gleaming lobby and are greeted by a smiling receptionist. You hand over a few personal and financial details, then take your card up to your room, swipe it, and flop down on the bed. You order room service, turn on the TV, and settle in for a relaxing evening.

Not everyone is cut out for Hotel Management, but there are few careers more rewarding than one that allows you to make everyone who walks through your doors feel valued and appreciated.

What according to us Hotel Management is?

• Hotel Management involves overseeing the administrative tasks of a Hotel or Resort. Your goal as a Hospitality Manager is to ensure your Hotel is warm, welcoming, and makes guests feel like they're at home.

• For Hoteliers, Hotel Management is not one concept but many tied together under one umbrella. It's hard to really say you've mastered Hotel Management when it comes with such a range of roles and responsibilities. Being able to adapt, meet challenges, and place yourself on a scale of personal growth is vital for a Hotel Manager.

• There are always new strategies, traveller preferences, or industry technologies emerging that you have to keep track of. Even new roles within hotels and the hotel industry are being created that will affect the way one manages their property so it pays to have your finger on the pulse.

The biggest question for every aspirants who want to pursue Hotel Management as an career is the difference between the Hotel Industry and the Hospitality Industry.

One common area of confusion relates to the difference between the Hotel Industry and the Hospitality Industry, with many people mistakenly believing the two terms refer to the same thing. However, while there is a cross-over, the difference is that the Hospitality Industry is broader in scope and includes multiple different sectors.

The Hotel Industry is solely concerned with the provision of guest accommodation and related services. By contrast, the Hospitality Industry is concerned with leisure in a more general sense. As a result, it covers Accommodation, Restaurants, Bars, Cafés, Night-Life and a number of travel and tourism services.

More specifically the difference between Hotel Management and Hospitality Industry can be discussed on three basic factors:-

1. <u>Area of Work</u>

• As the name suggests, HOTEL MANAGEMENT deals with all aspects of managing a hotel or more broadly, any lodging establishment such as a B&B, Resorts, etc. India, being an important tourism hub, is home to a large number of Hotels and Hotel chains. Hotel Management involves managing their day-to-day operations.

• HOSPITALITY MANAGEMENT, on the other hand, is a broader term used to describe any sector that deals with people management. It could be Casinos, Night Clubs, Conferences, Events, Sales, Business Development, and even Hotels.

2.Responsibilities

• The primary responsibilities, with Hotel Management, is ensuring guests enjoy a pleasant stay at their establishment. It involves taking care of them from the moment they checkin to the moment they check-out. Every single activity of the guest has to be outstanding to ensure their visit is worth their money.

• Similar to hotel management, hospitality management also includes taking care of guests, albeit in a different setting. For example, hospitality managers in large organizations are responsible for meeting and greeting foreign delegates and ensuring they have everything they need for a successful visit.

3.Driving Factors

• Hotel Management is largely an operations-oriented subject. Hotel managers mostly ensure each department in the hotel runs like a well-oiled machine. A Hotel Management degree, thus, provides intense training on how to manage these departments.

• Hospitality Management is about people management. The aim is to make sure guests are comfortable and satisfied with their experience at the Event, Venue, Hotel, etc. A good Hospitality Manager is one who takes customer/client experiences to the next level.

2

UNRAVEL (Reality of Hospitality)

"Don't take yourself too seriously, because we are not making rockets, comedown, chill and just enjoy the beautiful life that you have already chosen."

Can you choose Hotel Management as you career?

Firstly, those persons who posses the following characteristics, should not choose Hotel Management as their career:-

• Person who do not want to give up their **Comfort Zone.**

• Person who is having a lot of **Ego.**

• Person who cannot bear **Frustration.**

• Person who is very prone to **Home Sickness.**

• Person who doesn't have a bit of **Patience.**

• Person who wants their **Salary** to be in **Lacs**from their joining date and want an **Air Conditioned Cabin.**

If you possess any of these qualities or characteristics then please do not choose Hotel Management as your career.

In today's world each and everyone of us are doing some really great works and many social works too..... and we are in such industry where each and everyday we get to do some of the social works and many comes to be unique for us.

Now, I will be discussing some of the Myths related to this Industry and also the answers to those Myth's:-

1.Limited to Cooking and Serving Food and Beverages

It is true that food and beverages service is a part of hotel industry but it is not just restricted to that. Hotel Management courses, apart from these, also includes the Housekeeping Department that aims to provide a clean and comfortable living environment to the guest during their stay at a particular hotel, the Front Office which is an integral part in Inter Departmental Functioning and the overall smooth Management of the Hotel services. It includes every aspect of service and functioning that goes into ensuring a smooth stay for the guest, from check in to check out.

2.Restricted to Hotel Industry

• The vast job description of the Hotel Management industry has created the notion that it's and related jobs are the only aspect of Hotel and Hospitality Management field. That, however, couldn't be farther from truth. Hospitality Industry is a vast field with scores of other management industry encompassed within its scope. It includes, other things beside Hotel Management, such as, **Event Planning, Sales and Marketing, Accounting Departments, Mall or Multiplex Management** etc.

• And it doesn't stop here, a student who has earned a degree or diploma in Hotel Management can work in **Club Management, Hotels**and **Restaurants, Hospital Administration** and **Catering, Airline Catering**and **Cabin Services, Guest Houses, Cruise Ship, Forest Lodges, Hotel & Catering Institutes, Catering Departments like- Shipping Companies, Banks, Armed Forces**, and **Railways, Hotel & Tourism Associations**, and many more.

3.Meant for people who score less in school

It is a farce or taboo associated with almost all higher education courses apart from a select few in our country. In reality, Hotel and Hospitality Management Industry is as challenging a higher education course as any other. Sure we don't need rocket scientists but a good academic knowledge creates a strong foundation to build your career in. Some Hotel Management Institutes in India have an extensive course curriculum including Business Communication,

Geography, Accounting, Human Resource, Marketing, Multiple Languages, etc. The best colleges have a rigorous selection and screening process too.

4. The industry has bad average pay

Like any other industry, a graduate needs to be trained and gain work experience to build a solid experience foundation for them. Hence, they start out slow before ascending the ladder of both, post and pay. However, this is a fact common and true for all career paths. The average pay for a hospitality graduate starts from Rs. 15,000 and steadily increases to reach even lakhs with experience. It is a field, like any other field, where you need to build up your career and your income increases the higher you get.

5. It is a redundant career

Again, another myth that needs to be busted is the one that says Hotel Management is a redundant career path where you just end up being a glorified maid or man servant. It is a career where you get a lot of different opportunities to excel in your field while doing something you enjoy. Hotel Industry opens up the gates for you to work in five star hotels like Hyatt, Oberoi Group, Taj Group, Trident, etc. A hospitality graduate can also work in Casinos or Luxury Cruise Ships, giving them a well-paid as well as enjoyable career not only in India but also abroad.

6. Not good for Women

As far as the patriarchal saying goes, no job is good for women. Hospitality industry is one of the leading industries debunking and refuting this stigma. It is an industry where a woman's charming personality, calm-headedness and general observational and management skills are appreciated and promoted. This industry has seen a healthy increase in number of women holding high posts and is a great field for young female graduates to build their career.

7. Industry growth is less

This myth is frankly, laughable as the Hotel and Hospitality Industry is one of the fastest growing one. Tourism is a field that isn't about to see economical stagnancy anytime soon. This generates a lot of new opportunities for the related graduates with new job opening cropping up everywhere.

8.Hospitality and Hotel Management is the same thing

Hotel Management is not a synonym but a branch of the Hospitality Industry that includes Casino Management, Cruise Overseeing, Mall and Multiplexes, Event Management and many more.

9.Long Job Hour After Graduation

Indeed the Hotel Industry stays on every hour of every day throughout the year. However, this 24/7/365 working schedule, instead of being demanding and cumbersome gives you the opportunity to work according to your convenience. Prefer a 9 to 5 shift? The Hotel is open at that time. Prefer a night shift? The Hotel is still open at that time! Part time job? Yes, they need more staff during peak season!

10.Students are free labour

Most Hotel Management Institutes in India have their own Hotels or Workspace and the students are given a shift to work. However, this is not free labour but an integral part of their curriculum. The training they obtain from their colleges is going to be a star mark on their resume as they set out to start their career in the industry.

These myths will only matter to you if you possess the characteristics which are discussed at the starting of this lesson. Once you overcome these characteristics and these myths, then do believe that you can do wonders in this industry. No one can stop you from achieving your desired goal.

3

PHANTASM (Society's Perception)

SOCIETY! SOCIETY! SOCIETY!
(What he thinks, what she think,
what everyone in the society thinks!)

The word 'SOCIETY' is considered to be the most powerful weapon because of which most of the students of the world of different fields gets distracted and this results in their unsuccessful career. Especially in INDIA this word is given very high value and respect and hence the output is failure and unsuccessful careers .

The real truth is that which is hard to understand that we are not mislead or failed because of the society but we are failed because we accept the evil concepts and thinking of the society considering that truth which always results to the wicked thoughts in the mind of the student and ultimately leads to the failure in the goals.

What will the society think?

Has cleared many dreams!!

The biggest question:

Anyone of you ever observed why there is very less competition and awareness about Hotel Industry ?

Everyone knows about B. Tech, MBA, B. COM, SSC, BANK PO, etc.

But as we say 'Hotel Management' the faces of people are speechless but at the same moment 60% people start thinking 2 very negative words i.e.

-Waiter

-Bawarchi or Halwai

And this is the biggest problem with the mind-set of society, a very negative and small thinking about the Hotel Industry due to which we Hoteliers are too back in the society.

The society have very cheap thinking about the industry, they think that this creates mental pressure for a student which leads to failure.

Everything in life has a starting with "0" then with each step of experience you get promotion.

Unlike in this Industry, when you will work as a "Waiter" or an "Commi" or as a "Houseperson" you are going to develop skills and experience which will help you further in this Industry. Without working at these positions you cannot stabilise yourself for a longer time if you join this Industry.

If one wants to have a successful future, then please avoid distraction and negative thoughts and feelings given by the society because they are the biggest enemy of the student who wants to have wonders and successful future.

Our beautiful Hotel Industry is not about just being an Steward (Waiter) or an Halwai, it is much more than these words.

We all are updates with the new digital world and the technologies are very fast in the modern time. It is being the tagline of a successful hotelier that:

'Avoid what everyone think, focus on your work and you will do wonders in the future.'

One more reason of failure in Hotel Industry is that :

'Approx 90% students who have the thinking that 'What family members say! What cousins think!'

The biggest problem even we suffer that the son or the daughter of the relatives are well settled in different popular fields such as Engineering, Law, Government Jobs etc.

And as we say we want to pursue my career in the Hotel Industry and want to be an successful future Hotelier, at same time the parents started scolding and presenting various examples of other relative's children and started thinking that **'What will society and everyone think ! What about the goodwill and reputation of the family if we tell that my child wants to join Hotel Industry and wants to become an Steward. '**

It is not the fault of your parents or of my parents or of this society it is just because they also accepted the year's ago thought process of the people about this Industry.

Please! Please! Please!

·To all the upcoming future Hoteliers, it is your responsibility to understand the truth and fact about the Hotel Industry.

·You have to change the mind-set of your parents.

·You are the one to create an example in the society that this industry has infinite options to have a good career.

·This industry is just not being the Waiter or Chef, this industry is beyond the thinking of this society.

·We all have lots of chances of getting a bright future from this industry.

The most important message to all the upcoming future Hotelier will be just to stay focused on the work, avoid all distraction given by the society because usually we humans have tendency of feel jealous if someone is successful.

But the successful or winner overcomes all the distraction given by the society and moves forward because we have a passion for the work. The so called society is the one who speaks at the back, as the courage lacks they speak at back.

Mind your attitude according to you, not the society. Be confident in yourselves have passion in the work and you will be successful.

4

ACTUALITY (Student's Perception)

"Highly sensitive people are too often perceived as weaklings or damaged goods. To feel intensely is not a symptom of weakness, it is the trademark of the truly alive and compassionate. It is not the empath who is broken, it is society that has become dysfunctional and emotionally disabled. There is no shame in expressing your authentic feelings. Those who are at times described as being a 'hot mess' or having 'too many issues' are the very fabric of what keeps the dream alive for a more caring, humane world. Never be ashamed to let your tears shine a light in this world."

Hospitality Management Institutes have seen a tremendous growth in the recent years. More and more students are inclining to pursue Hospitality related course from the Institutes at National Level or at different Universities or from Private Institutes. The popularity of this course among the young aspirants is because of various factors such as, Job Opportunities, Different Avenues, Popularity of various Television Program based on Cooking Skills, Parents of Students already into Hotel Business, Entrepreneurship Plans, Overseas Job Opportunities, Passion and Interest, etc. Whenever a student takes admission to the Hospitality Course he does think positive about the Industry.

I have a lot of acquaintances asking me what motivated me to pursue a career in the Hotel and Tourism industry.

They would be better off asking me to define the purpose of life or explain astrophysics, because there is no clear and certain answer to that question. It all depends on what a person seeks from choosing to work in hotels.

5 big reasons why I chose this industry or why one should choose this industry:

1.<u>Hospitality has history...</u>

The emergence of Boutique Hotels in the last 15 years is a prime example of this. The changing tastes of travellers has led to ever more unique and personalised accommodation experiences. Now, instead of 100 rooms furnished by the same supplier, guests can have themed decor. Health and wellbeing is another new feature of these hotels, with gyms, health-conscious menus and even work out equipment in rooms. It's a clear message from consumers that innovation is key to success in hospitality.

The reasons are just about as vast as the industry and as deep as its roots in history. Historically, people travelled around and just as today the basic needs such as a warm bed and healthy meals had to be met. However, unlike ancient time, the industry has continuously evolved to its highest extents – and with future technologies and resources, promises to innovate more and more with each single client.

2.<u>A fast-growing future...</u>

Did you know that the Travel and Tourism Industry is the 21st Century's fastest growing Industry?

As mentioned before, the lodging industry can be traced way back in history, and will surely be present in the far future to come. If nearly 2,000 years ago, Nomads and Travelers used to "Check-In" at Inns and Huts, by the time you will finish reading this book the world will be just that much closer to establishing Hotels in space (think of the International Space Station). So not only is this Industry evolving, but with vacant rooms it brings vacant job posts as well.

These jobs are becoming ever more varied, with the traditional departments of Front Office, Housekeeping, Laundry, Concierge and Guest Relations seeing new additions. Fitness teams, Nutritionists and even in-house Designers are positions available in the modern Hotel Industry.

3.Diversity and Opportunity

Another reason is that Hospitality requires you to work in a multi-cultural environment. Working in a Hotel does not mean that Internationalism within the establishment stops at your clients; for the people behind the reception, in the kitchen and at the offices come from all corners of the world and they bring along with them their own language, cultural background and ideas on how to efficiently work within the Industry.

A key factor in this "Job Description" is to be able to communicate and work with different people from different backgrounds – as one big team.

4.It Gives You Room to Grow

The Hospitality Industry allows you to develop yourself – professionally and as a person. Not only do you improve on the professional skills you already possess, but with time and commitment you learn others due to the variety of colleagues, clients and situations that will put you to the test.

Various characteristics are required for working in a Hotel. Also, probably the most important matter is that you – literally – take care of people. This is debatable, but my experience tells me it takes empathy and commitment to put another person's needs and desires ahead of your own – while keeping a smile on your face.

5.It's just awesome!

Finally, the reason why I love Hospitality so much is simple: it's fun – as in enjoyable. All the dynamics, all the shifting with different responsibilities and the feeling you have when you start training and end up in a managing position, it's more than satisfactory at the end of the day. And it does not stop with the customer-facing part of the Hotel, you have the opportunity to meet and socialize with people representing a wide range of nationalities, in an even wider range of places all around the world.

In conclusion, **the Hotel Industry is a pretty interesting and pleasant domain to get involved in. As any other job, it has its ups and downs, and that's the great part of it: there is always place for innovation and there will always be innovators.**

5

PLIGHT (Initial Problems)

———◦♡◦———

" Problem is chance for you to do your best. "

We all in this world are filled with numerous problems in life. None of the us in this world is surviving without any cause or problem.

But it is also very true that "The one who overcomes or conquer all the problems is termed as a **Winner**or a **Successful Person.**

Even these problems brings lots of challenges in the human life.

Problems also do provide us lots of opportunities but totally it depends upon us how we tackle all the problems of life and keep the smooth going life.

Now the biggest questions arises that what all are the initial challenges that are faced by an Hotel Management Student?

·Firstly, the biggest challenge to make yours parents comfortable and familiarise with the course and let them understand the benefit sights of the course and make believe them that it is not just like what society thinks.

·The Second challenge and most important step where the most students suffer failure is that they are bounded with the "Distraction" (may be from society or from friends). So all you need to do is just to ignore these silly and useless things and move on because a small thing cannot result failure in your mission. You will be successful because you have the passion for your work.

·The third challenge is the entrance and choosing the right choice of college because your decision for right college will decide your bright future.

The NCHM (National Council for Hotel Management) conducts the exam every year which is a passage through which one can get the admission in the top IHM Colleges. There are 46 IHM's in INDIA and endless number of private institutes.

" If you have a desire to achieve,

make sure that you will achieve and

clear all the obstacles in between. "

Only these are not the challenges faced by an student, but an student also think about his/her college life some may be excited and some may be nervous.

Here are some points to conclude by which one must aware and have the idea what are the things that happen in the college life of an Hotel Management College Student.

The students have the biggest fear with the word 'Ragging'.

So it is an humble request from aspirants to be fearless as there is no ragging in the IHM's anymore.

Just for the interaction and familiarisation with the students, seniors conduct a normal introduction session for the very first week in the colleges just to make their juniors feel comfortable with the atmosphere of the college.

Most arising question from parents comes that, 'Is my child safe because this is for first time he is going out for studies?'

So it totally depends upon the student how they adjust with the other students, as many students comes from different regions of India so you have to be capable enough to tackle different people with pleasant and calm way.

60% students face the problem of 'Status Level'. The word is very complicated but the answer is very easy.

See, always remember not only in college but also in the entire life never judge yours status with anyone. No one is same in this world. It's better to always judge yourself rather than judging others because it creates misunderstanding and leads to distraction.

One of the very biggest problem face by Hotel Management Student is 'Food'. As many students comes from different regions so it creates problem, so no need to panic everything is provided in every state which is best at its quality and even in taste and with high nutritive value.

College life is full of fun, just enjoy your precious life but remember always choose correct path, fun is at its place and passion and desire is at it's place so manage accordingly.

So these were some of the important things you must know prior joining any Hotel Management College.

Always remember one thing in the life:-

'If there are problems, there are infinite solutions.'

All you have to do is to choose the correct path which have solutions and chase them as if you have a desire to earn something , then you will!

6

TRIUMPH (The Final Lesson)

—♡—

**SUCCESS COMES FROM
EXPERIENCE AND EXPERIENCE
COMES FROM EXPERIENCES.**

All we have learn from the previous all lessons is that we, the Hoteliers and all the upcoming future Hotelier are best and limitless. You all have the powers and passion towards the work.

All is what you have to execute your supreme power in the perfect direction without getting any sort of distraction.

Always remember society and other's will always be jealous with your success and distract you from achieving your goal, just maintain the focus and target on your goals, Believe no one can stop you from getting successful.

There are some important tips for all the future Hoteliers for getting successful:

·The most important thing is just believe in your work and yourself, I guarantee no one can stop you once you start believing yourself.

·**"Real happiness lies in making others happy. "**

If you follow this, surely the Hotel industry is for you and give you a bright future.

·One must always be polite and humble towards the people.

·Confidence and Attitude must be there to attain a bright future, but always remember over-confidence leads to failure.

·Must possessed with the helping attitude.

·Never count yourself in terms of the money.

·Avoid getting fear with the work, always let work to get fear from you , i.e. always enjoy the work and try to achieve all targets.

·What you are doing today pays you tomorrow. So plan accordingly and make each day of your life perfect.

· **'Speak less, listen more'** for being successful.

The truth of this industry hardly gets noticed by anyone that one Hotelier gets endless blessings throughout his tenure as we the hotelier are serving and helping people and are ready 24/7 for the service of our guests.

Did you notice?

Hotel is the place which is available 365 days (24/7) for general public. We believe in customer satisfaction and if customer is happy, we are happy.

So, at the end, a short message to all the upcoming future hoteliers:

You have the power which is hidden, all you have to do is to work on yourself and fund those extraordinary powers and work on it to make yourself a successful Hotelier in life.

We Hotelier are winners because we choose to serve people. And nothing makes you more happier if you make and feel others happy.

"Hard work always pays well ! "